the little book of
MIND
-LESS-
NESS

Published in 2014 by Carlton Books
an imprint of
the Carlton Publishing Group
20 Mortimer Street
London W1T 3JW

Copyright © 2014 Carlton Publishing Group

A CIP catalogue record for this book is available from the British
Library.

ISBN 978-1-78097-645-7

10 9 8 7 6 5 4 3 2

Printed in China

the little book of
MIND -LESS- NESS

don't try • disengage • care less

Giddy Knowall

CARLTON
BOOKS

A MINDLESS INTRODUCTION

Hello there, and thanks for entering my world of mindlessness. Welcome to the club.

Take off your shoes, put on some relaxing whale sounds or pan-pipe "music", and choose your favourite chair. Sit down and unwind. Close your eyes. Take a deep breath. Do as I say.

Or don't.

In fact, do whatever you want. I don't care. That's the great thing about mindlessness: you are free to behave as you wish. If you want to live your life the same way as everyone else – like a robot-zombie hybrid – then go for it. That behaviour is just as mindless as if you wanted to live your life acting without consequence, without thinking, meandering directionless for all eternity.

The beauty of mindlessness is that it *is* mindless. You, me – all of us – can behave both spontaneously

and routinely all at the same time if we wanted to –
how mindless is that?

Actually, you need to be mindful of that.

Modern "civilization" forces us to be mindful of
what we say, how we say it, and how we should
always be mindful of our actions and their
consequences. But that's simply not true. You can
do whatever you want, be whoever you want to be.
And you don't need me to tell you that. But because
you've bought my book, I should probably tell you
anyway – otherwise this book would be an even
more futile and mindless exercise in mindlessness
than it already is.

Enjoy!

Or not.

Whatever.

Before we begin, take a deep breath, switch off your brain and prepare your body for full-on mindlessness.

Don't turn the page until you're ready to make a complete start. Are you:

1. Bored out of your mind and have absolutely nothing better to do?

2. Willing to skim-read the words, not really taking any of it in?

3. Prepared to carry out some mindless behaviour afterwards?

4. Three glasses in to a bottle of wine?

Buying this book was your first step to mindlessness.

As you'll quickly learn, mindlessness can't be taught in any book.

Take this moment to pat yourself on the back, you've already completed Part One.

Your mindless adventure begins......................NOW!

The Meaning of Mindlessness

1. Acting without justification and with no concern for the consequences:
   e.g. "The rioters looting the fancy dress shop are mindless idiots – but they look hilarious."

2. (Of an activity) so simple or repetitive as to be performed automatically:
   e.g. "My boss wants me to perform a task so mindless even a zombie could do it – an actual creature of the undead."

3. (Mindless of) Not thinking of, or concerned about:
   e.g. "Mindless of the fact he was naked, he rushed to open the door to collect his Amazon delivery."

Judge a book by its cover – you're not going to read the damn thing anyway.

Try bringing more mindlessness into your routine aspects of your daily life:

- When having sex with someone you love

- When driving your car on a motorway

- When getting dressed in the morning

- When listening to your boss

There are endless possibilities of when to be disengaged and mindless throughout the day. When will you be mindless today?

Rules of mindlessness

1ST RULE: You don't talk about mindlessness.

2ND RULE: You don't think about mindlessness.

3RD RULE: If this is your first day of being mindless, you have to be the most mindless.

4TH RULE: No shirts or shoes allowed. Mindlessness has no uniform.

5TH RULE: Feel free to mindlessly break these rules.

Accept who you are

Every morning when you wake up, and every night when you get into bed, admit to yourself that you are a mindless person, mindlessly getting through the day and not really taking that much consideration into what you are doing or how you are doing it and not really caring what the consequences of those actions are. Be non-judgemental and compassionate about yourself and just accept that you are a dull and pointless human being who just blindly does what other people tell you to do... and embrace it!

The two problems with mindlessness:

1. You become bored of mindlessness – it can get quite mindless after a while.

2. You become mindless of mindlessness, effectively becoming mindful.

Listen to your inner voice – allow it to be heard...

(...then violently act out whatever it tells you to do.)

Take a few moments to ignore and forget whatever sounds and events are going on around you at this exact moment in time

- It could be a car horn, an elderly lady at a pedestrian crossing, people screaming "STOP"...

- Avoid focusing your awareness on these sounds – really drown them out, especially the police sirens.

- Whistle or hum a melodic tune, really drive the point home. Let nothing distract you.

Becoming mindless helps you:

- Grow detached from people and things you don't care about anyway.

- From noticing all the pointless incompetence and villainy in the world.

- Forget the never-ending life ambitions society forces you to achieve.

Online mindlessness

Facebook, Twitter and Instagram
are the most mindless activities you
can enjoy these days. Take some time out for
yourself right now. Log in to your profile now,
and spend three hours dutifully wasting your
time doing the following:

1. Taking comfort in an old school friend's
   weight gain.

2. Trawling through an ex-partner's
   wedding photos.

3. 'Liking' baby photos of people you haven't
   seen in over a decade.

4. Rewriting a status update or tweet so that
   it is smug but not too smug.

People who drive you to become more mindless every single day:

1. Your boss

2. Your family

3. That guy who gets on the train before everybody else gets off…

4. Anyone on TV who doesn't deserve to be there

5. Everyone, actually, when you think about it

When you go on a journey, be mindless of where you're going, how you're going to get there and what you need to take with you. Just walk out the door.

Remember: the only thing that is really important is that someone else ends up paying for it.

Mindless acronyms mindless people use mindlessly, number 7,352:

N R T F M

Never
Read
The
Flatpack
Manual

Mindlessness means never having to say sorry for anything you say or do.

If you feel yourself apologizing for your random acts of mindlessness, take a second, breathe deeply, check your iPhone for new emails and then LOL.

"Thinking is the hardest work there is... which is probably the reason so few engage in it."

HENRY FORD

Don't choose your battles.

Let your battles choose you.

"*The trouble with having an open mind, of course, is that people will insist on coming along and trying to put things in it.*"

TERRY PRATCHETT

Surround yourself with people who share your love of the pointless and the idiotic. They're good people.

From this point on, choose new friends recklessly and abandon the old. Invite people you've never met into the warm, secure confines of your own home.

Be the same as everyone else

Change all your online passwords to:

password

Change your home security combination to

1-2-3-4

Never be afraid to do the same as everybody else. It is your shared identity with your peers that makes you unique.

The key to achieving mindlessness is not trying to try and please everybody any of the time.

Let people know you are not afraid of wasting your own time in order to waste theirs.

If you want to know where your heart is, just look where your mind goes when it wanders.

You'll be pleasantly suprised!

Mindless acronyms mindless people use mindlessly, number 9,455,678:

Stop everything you're doing.

High-five your inner mindlessness.

Indulge your deepest, most darkest thoughts.

Take off your clothes.

Mindless maxim

As we grow older, we become more foolish *and* more wise.

(Only a mindless person could have said – and believed – this nonsense.)

Mindless careers

About 35.6 per cent of the world's workforce loathe their job. If you've had enough of working long hours for little pay, then fill out an application form for these mind-numbing jobs today and start a new mindless career:

a. Lifeguard
(you literally get paid to look at naked people)

b. Sports mascot
(you literally get paid to work in fancy dress)

c. Living statue
(you literally get paid to do nothing)

d. Ice cream man
(you literally drive round in a van all day serving ice cream)

e. Cat sitter
(you literally sit with a cat)

Apologies for the all-staffer

Everybody loves to hate mindless work emails; they unite the workforce by everyone collectively hating the sender. Send a pointless email to your colleagues today and start your day as you mean to go on:

From: You
To: All Staff
Re: Has anyone seen my mug?

Apologies for the all-staffer,
Has anyone seen my mug? It has a cat in a tutu on it, and I've marked my initials on the bottom of it with permanent marker.

If someone's using it without my permission, and obviously by mistake, please return it back to me immediately. You're not in trouble – I just can't have a cup of tea without it.

I'll leave my desk now for 10 minutes and whoever is responsible can leave it there anonymously.

Best, *Me*

Social media mindlessness

Facebook, Twitter and Instagram news feeds are now just filled up with meaningless status updates and vainglorious boasting. Don't pretend you're above it – get involved and join in. Fill up your friend's news feeds with your own tedious nonsense, such as:

@mindlessman78 Just saw a dog

@mindlessman78 Thank god it's Friday!!!!!!!!

@mindlessman78 Doctor just told me bad news ☹

@mindlessman78 Ooh, that dog's back

By sending mindless tweets such as these, you'll quickly discover who your real "friends" are.

Great mindlessness in football history

Each of these remarkable events should be remembered, and celebrated, as the world's most outstanding moments of sporting mindlessless. Take inspiration today:

1. David Beckham's red card for fouling Argentina's Diego Simeone, World Cup 1998. The most mindless foul ever on a football pitch?

2. Manchester United's Eric Cantona kung-fu kicking of a Crystal Palace fan in 1995. Priceless mindlessness.

3. Argentina's Maradona's "hand of god" against England in the 1988 World Cup. Unnecessary and pointless – brilliant stuff.

You know you're mindless when...

1. You can't remember if today is Tuesday or Wednesday.

2. You buy the same overpriced coffee from the same coffee shop simply because it's the closest one to your office.

3. You can't remember how you got to work.

Mindless things to do today to help kill the time at work

a. Spend your entire day at work quite literally staring at the clock.

b. Watch an entire movie on your iPhone while on the toilet.

c. Send the same email to the same person 250 times. Let them waste *their* time deleting it. Blame the 'gremlins' in your computer.

Don't be selfish

Don't keep your mindlessness all to yourself. Share it with the world by doing the following:

i) Pushing the emergency alarm on a crowded train

ii) Text your friends while driving

iii) Take a selfie while driving

iv) Write inappropriate comments underneath many YouTube videos

v) Use the term "WTF" in conversation

vi) Use the word "ironic" incorrectly

vii) Use the word "literally" incorrectly, but consider it OK because you've heard literally everyone else do it too.

37

Mindless acheivements

Even though mindlessness is about acting on a whim, or just doing things on autopilot, some mindless people find it best to compile a Top Ten To-Do list of their top mindless things they'd like to accomplish in their lifetime. A F**ket List, if you will.

Spend as long as you like staring out the window trying to think of things that you'd selfishlessly like to achieve.

(Mindless people tend to forget things so it's always best if you write these things down.)

How mindless are you feeling today?

1. You can't be bothered to go to work, so you might "work from home".

2. You're thinking of going to the airport and getting on the first flight you can afford.

3. You'll go to work, but you'll just phone it in and do as little as humanly possible, because you know no-one will notice.

4. You're going to hunt down and publicly destroy the first person who sends you an "Apologies for the all staffer" email.

Mindless mantras mindless people live their lives by:

a. Nothing ventured, nothing gained.

b. Two wrongs don't make a right.

c. Fortune favours the bold.

d. Better late than never.

e. You can't make an omelette without breaking some eggs.

f. Actions speak louder than words.

g. If you want something done right, you have to do it yourself.

Try and squeeze as many of these into your daily mindless conversations as possible, instead of coming up with anything original for yourself.

Mindless fonts to use when replying to serious and urgent work emails that you couldn't give two flying figs about:

1. COMIC SANS MS

2. **BRAGGADOCIO**

3. *MISTRAL*

4. **HAETTENSCHWEILER**

5. ☝✌✊❄📬✋☠💧👌✝☝✋🤚☹☝☼

If you're thinking outside the box,
you're trying too hard.

Think *inside* the box.

In fact, stop wasting time thinking of boxes.

Mindless workplace joke to use with the same colleagues every day:

"You don't have to be a mindless robot to work here... but it helps!"

Mindlessness[2]

Focus all your mindfulness onto the blank square opposite. Don't stop until you feel all of the day's intelligence and rational thinking drain away from your mind, to be replaced by blind obedience and thoughtlessness. Once you've finished, shake the book vigorously to waft away all that dreadful positive mindful energy. Your mind is now clear.

"When the time for action comes, stop thinking and go in."

NAPOLEON BONAPARTE

A mindless list of chores to do to distract you from important work:

I. Washing the car
II. Tidying the garage
III. Tidying your desk
IV. Ironing your underwear
V. Adding limescale to the kettle
VI. De-limescaling the kettle
VII. Making lists

*"If something's worth doing,
it's worth doing rihgt."*

PETER SERAFINOWICZ

 In a recent survey, the people crowned "the world's most mindless" are, in no mindful order:

a. Students

b. Bankers

c. People who go to work

d. Anyone who works for the Government

e. The Government

f. The retired

g. Writers

h. Retired writers

i. The insane

"*Thinking doesn't pay. It just makes you discontented with what you see around you.*"

MILAN KUNDERA

How to stay mindless

a. Befriend young people, preferably those in their late teens, or university students.

b. Keep up to date with the newest social media trends, and participate in them blindly without question.

c. Buy multiple copies of this book and keep a copy for every room of the house.

d. Go on a Mindless Diet (*see next page*).

The Mindless 5:2 Diet

One of the best techniques for keeping your mind as mindless as humanly possible is my renowned Mindless Diet. It's guaranteed* to make you mindless more quickly than any other diet. This celebrated diet involves 5 days of binge mindlessness followed by two days of mindfulness rest and recouperation.

All the celebrities are doing it – and in the true spirit of mindlessness, so should you.

*Not a legal guarantee

Mindful people to avoid today

a. Parents

b. Friends with children

c. Friends without children

d. Clergymen

e. Police

f. Doctors

g. Spouse

How to prove your mindlessness

a. Do something mindless right NOW, the more mindless the better.

b. Do it again.

c. Do it again.

c. Keep on doing it until you feel like you're doing it mindlessly.

d. See a).

A mindless task

Are you feeling really mindless today? Why not rip up all the really pointless "Mindful books" that litter the bookshops in to tiny unreadable pieces. Here's a few worthy titles to start off with:

1. *The Little Book of Mindfulness*

2. *365 Days of Mindfulness*

3. *Mindfulness: A Practical Guide to Finding Peace in a Frantic World*

4. *Mindfulness for Beginners*

5. *Advanced Mindfulness*

6. *The Complete Guide to Mindfulness*

7. *My, Aren't You Looking Mindful Today?*

Mindlessness and Marriage

Nothing proves how mindless you are more than getting married. But don't stop your mindlessness just because you get married – make sure you continue your mindlessness together until death do you both part.

a. Have mindless sex with mindless strangers – once you stop having meaningful sex with each other

b. Get stuck into a mindless routine with your spouse as quickly as possible (wearing pyjamas and binge-watching boxsets always speed this process up)

c. Be as mindless as possible when it comes to house chores, i.e. never empty the dishwasher, tidy away only your stuff, forget to wipe the toilet seat, etc...you know all this already, I bet

How to be mindlessness with money

The world may be suffering through a dizzying economic crisis, but that doesn't mean you have to stop being mindless with your own money.

1. Keep all your money in a black bin bag under your bed.

2. Ask for your monthly salary to be paid in cash.

3. Exhange all your money into Bitcoin.

4. Throw brown coins away.

5. Keep gold coins in a large glass container by an open window – where passersby can see it easily.

6. Buy Lottery tickets and scratchcards everyday.

Mindless statistics

According to a recent mindless survey on mindlessness, 15 per cent of the respondents wished they were more mindless. The remaining 85 per cent of people drew penises on the questionnaire.

"If you spend too much time thinking about a thing, you'll never get it done."

BRUCE LEE

"There is nothing either good or bad but thinking makes it so."

WILLIAM SHAKESPEARE

 Things mindless drivers never think about:

1. Cyclists

2. Parking inbetween the designated lines at Tesco

3. Lane discipline

4. Car insurance

5. Mirror, signal, and the other one

6. Parking in disabled spaces (regardless if it's "only just for a couple of minutes")

"Happiness is the longing for repetition."

MILAN KUNDERA

"Happiness is the longing for repetition."

MILAN KUNDERA

Mindlessness-by-numbers

If you're close to achieving these required minimum government statistics, it means you're approaching above-average mindlessness:

a. More than 6 hours of TV a day

b. More than three units of alcohol a day

c. More than three hours of social media a day

d. More than 3,000 calories a day

e. Less than 15 minutes of exercise a day

f. Less than two books a year
(and that doesn't include this one)

At first, mindlessness can seem like a lot of hard work and effort. However, after practising mindlessness for more than two minutes you should get the hang of it, and it'll come easily after that.

Be aware of your surroundings, work out how to maximize your mindlessness and drift off into a state of worry-free semi-consciousness. The more you do it, the more mindless you will become.

Mindlessness is like riding a bike. You never forget how to do it.

(And if it needs maintenance, just pay someone to fix it.)

Un-focus your mindlessness

- Throw your mindlessness about with wild abandon, don't think about it too much, if at all.

- Rush into it with little thought or direction and, most importantly, with indifference towards the consequences.

- Disengage your brain from the moment; act as if you're a five-year-old.

- Practising mindlessness, creating a care-free environment that is free of rational ideas, is conducive to haziness of thought.

Throw your hands in the air,
like you just don't care."

EVERY DJ EVER

The essence of mindlessness

It is easy to read about the importance of being mindless and then mindlessly forget to be mindless. And, actually, that's fine. That's just being downright mindless.

Opening this book at any page will give you all the ingredients you require to *remember* to be mindless. As you develop your mindless skills, you will start to not care about how mindless they are for you. Your relationships with people you actively don't care about will happily fade away, you will find mindless enjoyment in mindless activities, you will not yearn for things that require you to engage with other humans, such as strategy meetings, performance reviews and weddings. In short, reading these words is a pivotal moment in your life – in an instant all the things that you used to care about, will cease to exist, and your whole life and outlook will improve instantly. How do you feel?

Mindlessness makes you better than everybody else.

Keep this in mind next time you leave the house.

"My biggest fear is mindlessly and stupidly repeating myself."

JOHN LYDON, ON NOT BEING MINDLESS

"I like crazy people, especially those who don't see the risk."

JOHN LYDON, ON BEING MINDLESS

"Try not. Do or do not. There is no try."

YODA

Be judgemental of others – but only if it affects your ability to be mindless.

Don't let other people's mindfulness affect your mindlessness.

"Everything I do, I do with reckless abandon."

JOLENE BLALOCK

"Do not take life too seriously. You will never get out of it alive."

ELBERT HUBBARD

Commuting to mindlessness

Every day we get up and go to work. But don't just be mindless at work – start your mindlessness earlier and do it on the way there:

a. Spend three times longer in the shower than necessary so that your partner/flatmate ends up late and has goes to work unclean.

b. Turn your music up really loud on the train.

c. Shout "Can you move down, please?"to the person standing next to you, even if the train isn't crowded.

d. Buy the smelliest food known to man. Scoff it happily on the train.

e. Read aloud the newspaper of the person who you sitting next to. Read out the page ahead of them for extra mindlessness.

In 2014, the National Union of Mindless Bureacracy (NUMB) endorsed the teaching and clinical trials carried out at the Behaviour of Utter Mindlessness Society (BUMS) as an effective treatment against mindfulness and the prevention of rational thinking. Research has shown that people who have been mindful for 20 years or more, find that taking part in the studies carried out at BUMS reduced their levels of mindfulness in the body by upto 38 per cent.

People can benefit from mindlessness whether they have a specific mindful problem or not ... reducing our own awareness of other people's problems is the first step in maximizing mindlessness.

Mindlessness strips us of our consciousness and coherent thought, it takes us back to our raw, primal behaviours. Rely on your gut instincts today – *what's the worst that could happen?*

"*When you pay attention to boredom, it gets unbelievably interesting.*"

JON KABAT-ZINN

"At a time like this, we cannot afford the luxury of thinking!"

AYN RAND

You are only as mindless as your last act of mindlessness.

Be mindful of that the next time you decide to be mindless.

But don't be too mindful of it, obviously.

"The only means of strengthening one's intellect is to make up one's mind about nothing – to let the mind be a thoroughfare for all thoughts."

JOHN KEATS

Just do it...

or...

Don't do it.

Feeling mindless? Don't just sit there and think about it. Don't think about it all. Put some trousers on and go and do it.

You may regret it – but we'll cross that bridge then.*

*The Little Book of Regret *by Giddy Knowall is available from all good book shops.*

Invite mindlessness into your life by taking advantage of every opportunity:

1. While you're waiting for the kettle to boil, act out a mindless fantasy in your mind.

2. While your computer re-boots after crashing, do something without thinking.

3. Strike while the iron's hot – when doing the ironing.

4. Shout a mindless stream of unpleasantries down the phone while you're on hold with your internet provider.

5. When upon the toilet, do something mindless.

Mindless culture

Being mindless doesn't mean you shouldn't be cultured too. Go to an art gallery or museum every now and then. But go with a mindless attitude:

1. Just wander around aimlessly.

2. Don't go and see anything specific.

3. Don't read any of the little placards telling you any important information.

4. Don't join a guided tour.

5. Don't put on the headphones... or take any notes of any kind.

6. Definitely use the bathroom before you leave.

7. Try and finish in under 10 minutes.

There is a difference between giving-up and strategic disengagement.

Know the difference.

Keep an eye on your own mindlessness:

a. Set aside time to think about your own mindlessness and how to improve on it.

b. Choose a time when you know you will be distracted and unable to focus on it too clearly, i.e. putting the kids to bed, piloting a plane.

c. Feel bad about not thinking about it.

d. Put it off until a later date.

e. Don't do it then either.

Disengage your brain

Let your mind "work from home" today.

When it comes to mindlessness, practice doesn't make perfect. Mindlessness can be achieved perfectly first time every time.

Mindlessness is a state of mind. Terms and conditions do not apply.[1]

[1] no refunds allowed

Mindlessness isn't about bottling up your emotions.

Imagine for a moment you are a metaphorical "message-in-a-bottle" washed up on the sea shore. The "message" is you, OK. The 'bottle' is *your* life. Outside the bottle, the beach looks amazing – lots of attractive people drinking cocktails, wearing very little, blazing hot sun, and clear blue seas. You don't want to be contained in the bottle, do you? On the inside, forever looking out. You want to be outside, no longer looking in. No matter what your metaphorical "message" is – whether it's hate, panic, indifference, rage, incompetence or boredom – you just want to be free. All you have to do is push your way out; knock the cork out from the top. But don't waste time negotiating with the cork, talking to it, or trying to sneakily slip out against the slide. Don't bother wasting your time with all that. Be mindless. **SMASH THE GLASS.**

Mindlessness doesn't understand metaphors.

Let your mindlessness do all the talking today.

Identify an accessory upon your person that you use everyday – a watch, smartphone, credit card, for example – to which you can attribute "mindlessness".

Throughout the day, when you look at or use this particular object, let it instantly log you in to the unsecure, dark, and vacant area of your brain.

Now do something mindless.

For example, if your credit card is your "trigger", when paying a bill at a restaurant, get up and run away as quickly as possible. Don't look back.

Do something mindless now

Rip this page out, and eat it. What does that mindlessness taste like?

Mindless sleeping

Being mindless all day can often leave the body exhausted, but the mind totally awake. In order to achieve maximum mindlessness tomorrow, you need to have a decent amount of sleep today.

Mindlessness enjoys the routine of counting sheep. The repetition of watching those furry little lumps jump fences is enough to quiet even the most mindless of minds. Here's how to do it my guaranteed mindless way:

1. Lie down in bed. Let your whole body sink into whatever you're lying on.
2. Close your eyes. Breath deeply.
3. Imagine you're alone in a field. Imagine a fence in the distant. Walk towards the fence, but not too close.
4. Now imagine the once empty field to be full of white (or black) sheep.
5. Touch some of the sheep. Feel their soft hair on your hand. Doesn't it feel dreamy?

6. Now form the sheep into an orderly queue. Imagine them with numbers on their backs.
7. Picture a field full of millions of individual sheep all numbered.
8. Stand back from the fence.
9. Look at Sheep #1. Look at how excited she looks to please you.
10. Now, on your command, let Sheep #1 jump over the fence.
11. Felt good, didn't it?
12. Now focus on Sheep #2. Leave about five seconds per sheep. Watch them walk up to the fence, and then slowly jump over the fence.
13. Repeat until you're asleep.

Never be mindlessly idle

1. While standing in a queue for a ticket at a train station (or waiting for a friend), resist the urge to use that time wisely. Just stand there, mindless. Don't think of anyone or anything.

2. That said, if you feel like doing something even more mindless, then perhaps shout the word "FIRE" very loudly. The queue may end up being much shorter.

Mindless people have more electrical activity in their right frontal cortex of their brain, apparently. To stimulate this electrical activity even further, stick a fork up your nose. The act is so mindless that it will send your mind into a mindless rage.

Five reasons why mindlessness is better than mindfulness.

1. It's much more fun.

2. It requires much less forethought and organization.

3. It doesn't have to involve clothing.

4. You can do it anytime or anywhere you wish

5. If you do it right, you may even get a free ride in a police car.

6. You don't need a sixth reason.

Mindlessness extends beyond the reaches of your front door. Take a mindless trip to your local supermarket and indulge in pointless behaviour. It's easy:

a. Have 50 items in your basket when queuing at a "6 items or less" checkout.

b. Park your trolley full of items at a self-service checkout. Begin unloading.

c. Walk round the shop talking loudly, and aggressively, on your phone about how "people who stand in my way are gonna get it".

d. See how many vegetables you can steal before being escorted off the premises.

e. Don't swipe your loyalty card (unless you don't feel loyal to them, in which case, do)

Be even more mindless at work

Modern offices are a breeding ground for mindlessness. Make sure you increase your productivity for tedium every opportunity you have.

You can do this by never spell-checking any of your emails and talking like a robot – binary is the most impressive – when anyone ever commands you to do something they think is important.

Add more routine into your routine

Routine has a bad reputation, but when it comes to mindlessness, nothing helps you achieve your potential more than undemanding monotony.

Look around your workspace today – how can you inject more tediousness into your day?

Work meetings

The epitome of mindlessness, work meetings are full of saying and doing the same thing week in, week out, but never actually achieving anything. There is always room for improvement, however. Try these certified techniques:

a. Stare off into the middle distance, disengage with all conversation.

b. Yawn loudly whenever your boss begins to talk.

c. Stand up and shout "Yes!" when the meeting is finally over.

d. Draw genitalia on your notepad, and then point them out proudly to colleagues.

e. Whenever you hear corporate jargon, spin around in your chair.

How to be mindless at Christmas

Chances are you already carry out these techniques religiously, but it's always good to refresh your knowledge of them:

i.   Have your first alcoholic drink at 6 a.m.

ii.   Watch TV all day, despite everything being a repeat

iii. Spend hours cooking the same meal you have done ever year, only to be incredibly dissatisfied when it's finished, and receive little to no praise

iv.   Be incredibly thankful for socks, deodorant and bath gel

v.   Smile politely every time someone says, "You're so difficult to buy for..."

vi.   Buy a dog. But take it back on Boxing Day, claiming "It doesn't work"

In these digital days, there are so many devices that are designed to distract us from finding "peace and quiet". To keep all elements of peace and quiet from distracting you, put aside three hours a day when you speak on your phone, listen to the radio, watch TV and surf online – *all at the same time*. This will help your mindlessness grow.

Mindless places to go shopping with your partner

1. IKEA

Reasons why mindless jobs are the best

Whether it's data entry, telesales or just a bog-standard office job, working while using as little brain function as possible is the future of steady employment. Here's why:

1. Little responsibilty.

2. The broadband's better than at home.

3. Everyone else appears as unproductive as you wish to be.

4. You can leave on time all the time.

5. You do the same thing everyday.

6. Motivation and enthusiasm by your team to do a "good job" appears to have walked out the door years ago.

> *"I never came upon any of my discoveries through the process of rational thinking."*

ALBERT EINSTEIN

Untitled folder

A good way to mindlessly start your working day is to create 50 folders on your desktop all labeled "untitled folder".

Dump all your work in these different folders at random.

Every morning guess which folder that day's work is in.

At the end of each day, move the folders about.

This will kill about three hours a day mindlessly.

A simple six-step guide to mindlessness

1. Think of something mindful – and then do the exact opposite.

2. Don't think of anything mindful – just do the first thing that pops into your head.

3. Mindlessness gets better with routine. So, keep being mindless.

4. Be mindless when it's most inconvenient with other people.

5. If something feels boring or unnecessary, chances are it's mindless.

6. If someone calls you "stupid", or insults you in general, you're being mindless.

Don't be deceived by false mindlessness

You may feel like you're learning when you're watching TV quiz shows, but don't worry, you're not. They're just as mindless as other TV shows.

Many people will try to deceive you into thinking they are mindful people. Don't believe them. They're just as mindless as you.

"Alcohol.
The cause of, and solution to,
all of life's problems."

HOMER SIMPSON

Modern mindlessness

Don't risk being arrested for mindless vandalism on the street. Instead, mindlessly – and anonymously – grafitti some of Wikipedia's online pages instead. It's mindless fun that you don't have to leave your house for.

Mindlessness on the move

Go for a run, with no direction in mind – just follow your feet. While on this journey, carry out three mindless acts to get your heart pumping even more. I suggest the following:

1. Steal a piece of fruit or vegetable from outside the local shop.

2. Rip off the licence plate of a fancy car, then post it through their neighbour's letterbox.

3. Run into a local place of worship and exclaim: "Come out, come out, wherever you are."

4. Play knock and run on every house that looks nicer than yours.

"*You are thought here to be the most senseless and fit man for the job.*"

WILLIAM SHAKESPEARE

History of mindlessness

Mindlessness was one of the first behaviours adopted by Neanderthals, an early species of humankind. Neanderthals walked the earth around 500,000 years ago, but can still be spotted today on High Streets, and in places of work, all over the world.

Take inspiration from your ancestors today.

Everywhere you look today – no matter where you go – you will see mindlessness. Observe it. Watch it happen. Get aroused at the thought that you are not the only person being mindless today.

Take a minute to unfocus

We are all so busy in our pointless lives that's it's time for us to just stop for a second, take a deep breath and clutter our mind with mindless thoughts.

- Look at the second hand of a clock and watch one minute go by.

- After the minute ends, keep looking at the clock until an hour goes by.

- After the hour ends, keep looking at the clock until the day goes by.

- Try it now – to get a sense of time, and how it's OK to waste time mindlessly.

Live in the present moment.

But not that one...

This one!

Is your house untidy? Good.
Keep it that way.

An untidy house is an untidy mind.

Cultivate mindlessness

1. Go to your local garden centre.

2. Buy a plant of your choice.

3. Take it home and put it somewhere dark and dry.

4. Spend five minutes a day looking at it.

5. Never water it.

6. Watch it die slowly.

Use this technique to focus your thoughts on just how mindless life can be.

Mindless mornings matter

Mornings can be packed with mindlessness – if you just take your time.

Instead of rushing out the door, because you've overslept and you're late for work: slow down.

Take a moment to be mindless before the day is taken away from you.

Say yes to everything today.

Say no to everything today.

Revert back to your inner child

Answer "Why?" to every question you are asked today.

"Why?"

Exactly.

Mindless politics

It's not just us normal people who aspire to be mindless. Looking through history makes it apparent that mindlessness can seriously affect world leaders past and present too.

Spend time at work reading the Wikipedia biographies of presidents, prime ministers and politicians and take inspiration from their real acts of gratuitous mindlessless that ended up changing the world.

What mindless act would you do if you were in charge of the world?

Mindless haiku?

People who are mindful always have their mind's full.

People who are mindless, always mind less.

It's true, ¾ of mindless people don't think about the other ¼.

But then, ⅞ of mindless people don't think about fractions either.

Remember: Mindless people don't care enough to work stuff out.

Mindlessness doesn't need to quote
Lao Tzu to make its point.

*"Stop thinking,
and end your problems."*

LAO TZU

Instant mindlessness

Sometimes it takes us the whole day to achieve mindlessness. But with this non-certified technique you can be guaranteed to go from mindful to mindless in under five seconds:

1. Close your eyes.

2. Clear your mind.

3. Don't think about anything.

4. Don't move.

5. Stay that way for hours.

Just like that, you have achieved 100 per cent mindlessness. Try this at home now!

If you're feeling mindful, book an appointment to see your local mindless friend immediately. Don't suffer with mindfulness alone – there is a cure.

It is estimated that 75 per cent of all mindfulness can be treated within an hour of diagnosis.

 When you can feel your mindfulness levels rising:

i. Find a mirror.

ii. Take a long hard look at yourself.

iii. Give yourself a slap.

iv. Continue slapping yourself until you feel the mindfulness drain away.

Raise local awareness

1. Don't be selfish with your mindlessness.

2. Start a local Mindlessness club.

3. Get a group of mindless people together and discuss mindless things.

4. Spread the Mindless word online, like many popular websites, such as Facebook, do.

5. Having like-minded people on the shared mindlessness journey will encourage us all to continue practising mindlessness until it becomes even more widespread.

At ego non amens,
ergo ego sum.

(I don't think I'm mindless,
therefore I am.)

"*The best way to live in the moment is to ignore the moment is happening.*"

RANDOLPH WILSON

Mindless eating

1. Take a piece of fruit that takes ages to peel – a mango, for example.

2. While you peel the skin of the mango away from the juicy insides, reflect on how amazing nature is to give this piece of fruit a protective piece of packaging.

3. Be aware of all the hardships and beating-of-the-odds nature had to endure just to produce this piece of fruit. Think about the journey of the seed, the earth, the weather, the crop pickers, the international travel, the carbon footprint, yadda yadda, etc.

4. Look at the fruit. Stare long and hard at it. Become one with the fruit.

5. Throw the fruit in the bin.

6. Eat chips. With salt on.

Focus on the now

Don't be mindless in a minute.

Stop thinking about what happened a few minutes ago.

Stop waiting for a better moment to be mindless.

Start being mindless now.

And now.

And now.

And now.

And now.

And now.

And now.

And now... you get the picture.

Commit to mindlessness

A good friend of mine, John Poppycock, is a full-time master of mindlessness. He turned his mind to chaos and acting without consequence in the 1970s in order to demystify mindlessness, to make it accessible and relevant.

In a recent interview, he claimed that 2–4 weeks of practising a minimum of 30 minutes of mindlessness on a daily basis is enough to see radical and positive changes in one's life. As with every mindless commitment to a routine – there has to be discipline.

Blindly follow this guide, and you'll be mindless in mere minutes.

"If I decide to be an idiot, then I'll be an idiot on my own accord."

JOHANN SEBASTIAN BACH

"There's a fine line between fishing and just standing on the shore like an idiot."

STEVEN WRIGHT

As well as practising mindlessness, you may find it helpful to participate in other tasks that require very little thought:

1. **Watching daytime TV**. Participants sit silently and gaze blankly at a TV screen, watching presenters who aren't likeable enough to be on prime-time trying to educate people on antiques, selling houses and/or interior decorating.

2. **Socialising with friends.** Participants visit a pub and sit silently as they all interact with people who are in other pubs with other friends on their phones instead of each other, while drinking overpriced, unhealthy, addictive alcoholic drinks for no purpose whatsoever.

3. **Getting married.** Participants decide that they require to needlessly inject life back into a tired relationship and the most expensive, narcissistic and statistically lamentable way to do that is to commit publicly to a person who you're actually beginning to resent... until you die.

The Final Word:

Mindfulness can kill.